CHESAPEAKE BAY

by Leah Kaminski

CHERRY LAKE PUBLISHING • ANN ARBOR, MICHIGAN

Published in the United States of America by:

CHERRY LAKE PRESS

2395 South Huron Parkway, Suite 200, Ann Arbor, MI 48104
www.cherrylakepublishing.com

Reading Adviser: Marla Conn MS, Ed., Literacy specialist, Read-Ability, Inc.

Series Adviser: Amy Reese, Coordinator of Elementary Science; Howard County School
System, MD; President of Maryland Science Supervisors Association

Book Design: Book Buddy Media

Photo Credits: ©coastalpics/Getty Images, cover (front top), ©Rainer Lesniewski/Getty Images, cover (map),
©krb2002/Pixabay, cover (back), ©Pixabay, cover (red circle), ©Marilyn Barbone/Shutterstock, cover (bottom right),
©iStockphoto/Getty Images, 1, ©jopelka/Shutterstock, 3 (right), ©Lone Wolf Photography/Shutterstock, 3 (left),
©iStockphoto/Getty Images, 4, ©FrankRamspott/Getty Images, 6, ©iStockphoto/Getty Images, 7, ©Crystal Eye
Studio/Shutterstock, 8, ©Cameron Davidson/Getty Images, 9, ©iStockphoto/Getty Images, 10, ©Aurora Open/Getty
Images, 11, ©iStockphoto/Getty Images, 12, ©iStockphoto/Getty Images, 13, ©Flickr/Virginia State Parks, 14, ©pixel-
mixer/Pixabay, 15 (top), ©reptiles4all/Shutterstock, 15 (bottom), ©iStockphoto/Getty Images, 16, ©S2Photography/
Getty Images, 17, ©divedog/Shutterstock, 18, ©iStockphoto/Getty Images, 19, ©iStockphoto/Getty Images, 20,
©iStockphoto/Getty Images, 21 (top), ©Vicki Jauron, Babylon and Beyond Photography/Getty Images, 21 (bottom),
©Alexander Spatari/Getty Images, 22, ©Aurora Open/Getty Images, 2 , ©Ariel Skelley/Getty Images, 24, ©Aurora
Open/Getty Images, 25, ©Alex Wong/Getty Images, 26, ©iStockphoto/Getty Images, 27 (bottom), ©ribeiroantonio/
Shutterstock, 27 (top), ©Boristrost/Pixabay, 28 (glass), ©iStockphoto/Getty Images, 28 (food color), ©Mai Vu/
Getty Images, background (pattern), ©Devanath/Pixabay, (paperclips), ©louanapires/Pixabay, (paper texture)

Library of Congress Cataloging-in-Publication Data has been filed and is available at catalog.loc.gov

Cherry Lake Publishing would like to acknowledge the work of the Partnership for 21st Century Learning, a
Network of Battelle for Kids. Please visit *http://www.battelleforkids.org/networks/p21* for more information.

Printed in the United States of America
Corporate Graphics

CONTENTS

CHAPTER 1

The Systems of the Chesapeake Bay

Everything on Earth belongs to one of four major systems. They are called spheres. The **geosphere** relates to land, the **hydrosphere** relates to water, the **biosphere** relates to living things, and the **atmosphere** relates to air. These four Earth systems work together to create humans' living conditions. In this way, soil, water, air, and animals affect each other and the health of the entire Chesapeake Bay.

Glaciers melted to form rivers 18,000 years ago. It took the rivers thousands of years to flow to the Atlantic Ocean. The Susquehanna River reached the shore 10,000 years ago. Water levels rose and filled the plain around it. This flooded plain was the Chesapeake Bay.

The bay is off the coasts of Virginia and Maryland. It is around 200 miles (321 kilometers) long and between 3 and 30 miles (5 and 48 km) wide. Its western shore has cliffs. The low and marshy Delmarva Peninsula creates the bay's eastern shore. The bay's average depth is only 21 feet (6.4 meters). This is shallow compared to many other bays. For example, San Francisco Bay's average depth is 43 feet (12 m).

* Water, earth, and sky are home to many animals in the Chesapeake Bay, such as the Great Blue Heron.

The bay's hydrosphere contains the bay and the rivers that flow into it. Half of the bay's 18 trillion gallons (68 trillion liters) come from the Atlantic Ocean. Half come from the land and rivers. This mixture of saltwater and freshwater is called **brackish** water. This water makes the Chesapeake Bay an **estuary**. An estuary is a partly enclosed body of water where rivers enter the sea. Many bays are estuaries. The Chesapeake Bay is the largest estuary in the United States.

The bay's water has many different **habitats**. The land around the bay is called its watershed. It also has many habitats. Some of the main habitats are forests, **wetlands**, beaches, and open water. Every habitat serves different purposes for the health of the bay. Together they make up the bay's biosphere. Humans are part of the biosphere too. Around 18 million people live around the bay.

* Wetlands clean the bay's water and provide food and shelter for its animals.

The atmosphere of the bay is affected by warm sea breezes and ocean water. Its winters are cold but never freezing. Snow is rare. Summers do not get very hot on the bay's coast.

The **airshed** is the region of air above the bay. It affects the land and water beneath it. The rain that falls into the bay comes from the airshed. The Chesapeake Bay's airshed is nine times bigger than its watershed. Its air can come from as far as Canada.

The atmosphere can affect the other spheres in the bay. For example, rain washes **pollution** from the air into the bay's water. Pollution then affects the habitats of the bay. All of these systems are connected.

CHAPTER 2

The Chesapeake Bay Watershed

The land and rivers that drain into the Chesapeake Bay create its watershed. The Chesapeake Bay watershed covers 64,000 square miles (165,759 sq km). It has 11,684 miles (18,803 km) of shoreline. The shoreline includes islands. This is more shoreline than the entire West Coast of the United States.

Watershed Diagram

The watershed stretches south from lakes in upstate New York. It extends east from mountain streams in Virginia. All the water of this landmass drains into the waters of the bay.

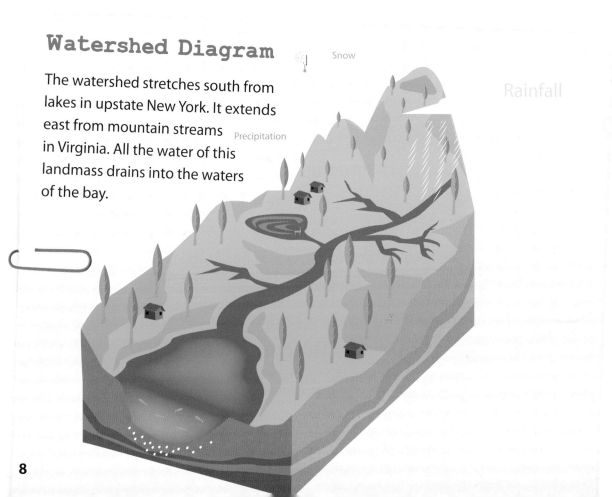

Snow

Rainfall

Precipitation

Rivers and creeks give water to the land around them as they move toward the bay.

More than 100,000 rivers and streams flow through the watershed. The Susquehanna, Potomac, Rappahannock, York, and James Rivers are the five largest rivers. Water from these rivers flows directly into the bay. This means what happens on land affects the water. For example, the forests and wetlands of the watershed protect the bay's water. They filter pollution through the ground. They stop polluted **runoff** from entering the water.

The water flowing into the bay can be described by its salinity, temperature, and circulation. Salinity is the amount of salt in the water. Temperature measures the water's hotness or coldness. Circulation is how the water flows.

The Chesapeake Bay is saltier near the ocean and fresher near the land, where water flows from the watershed. Also, salinity in the bay is different at different depths. Saltwater from the ocean is **denser** than freshwater from rivers. This means that the saltwater sinks. The bay is fresher at its surface and saltier at the bottom.

* The bay never freezes entirely, but in winter there can be chunks of ice on the surface.

The amount of mixing in the water changes by season. Cold water is denser than warmer water. When the water cools in fall and winter, it sinks and there is more mixing. In spring, warmer water floats and there is less mixing.

Water temperatures in the bay change a lot. The bay cannot hold heat because it is so shallow. The water can be 34 degrees Fahrenheit (1 degree Celsius) in winter and 84°F (28.8°C) in summer. Surface waters are warm in summer, while lower layers are cold.

★ During summer, the water is warm enough for many fun activities.

Circulation is created by the movement of freshwater from the watershed into the bay. It is also created by the sinking of cold water and by tides. Where different types of water mix together, oxygen and **nutrients** also mix. This creates important places for animals and plants. They depend on the oxygen and nutrients.

CHAPTER 3

Plants and Animals of the Chesapeake Bay

The Chesapeake Bay and its watershed are home to 3,600 species, or kinds of plants and animals. There are 348 fish species and 173 **shellfish** species. The bay's water is protected from strong ocean waves and tides, so it is calm. This makes the water safe for many animals and their food.

* Great blue herons are just one of many birds that are important to the bay's ecosystem.

* The Maryland blue crab has long been an important part of local food culture.

There are many kinds of birds in the bay. Gulls and terns eat at the edge of the water. Piping plovers and other small birds hop along the sand. Islands are cut off from **predatory** animals. Herons, bald eagles, and osprey rest there. About one-third of the **migrating** birds of the whole Atlantic Coast spend winter at the bay. Some of these are the common loon and tundra swan. In winter, almost 1 million water birds feed in the bay's wetlands.

Dolphins, seals, and sharks swim in the open waters of the bay. Bluefish, American shad, and bay anchovy live there too. Blue crabs are an important local species. Blue crabs have bright blue claws and green shells. The bay is famous for them. Many people catch and eat them.

There are also many **anadromous** fish in the bay. Anadromous fish are fish who spend their adult lives in the ocean but must lay eggs in the freshwater rivers of the watershed. They swim into the rivers in huge groups to lay eggs. They raise their young in the protected waters of the rivers, streams, and wetlands. Anadromous fish of the bay include striped bass (rockfish), perch, Atlantic sturgeon, and alewife.

Tiny plants and animals called plankton float in the water. Plankton are food for many other animals. The water also supports oysters. They filter nutrients, **sediment**, and pollution out of the water. This helps keep it clean. Oysters also create reefs at the bottom of the bay. Sponges, sea squirts, and small crabs live on their hard surfaces.

Sturgeons are the largest fish native to Chesapeake Bay. They are now very endangered.

Sika deer are a small, non-native elk species. They feed at night from the grasses of forested wetlands and marshes.

Forested areas have sika deer, black bears, coyotes, red and gray foxes, and groundhogs. Turtles such as the diamondback terrapin live in the rivers and water near the shore. Muskrats and beavers depend on the wetlands.

* Diamondback terrapins are native to the Chesapeake Bay area. They are Maryland's official state reptile.

The Chesapeake Bay watershed supports 2,700 types of plants. Plants such as smooth cordgrass, saltmeadow cordgrass, and marsh elder live in wetlands by the shore. Forested wetlands are seasonally or permanently flooded forests. Trees such as red maple, river birch, Atlantic white cedar, and bald cypress grow there. Shrubs such as willows and alders grow there too.

Just under two-thirds of the wetlands in the Chesapeake Bay watershed are forested.

Eelgrass is most common in the saltier water of the lower bay. It cannot grow in waters that are too warm.

Bay grasses live underwater. Fourteen varieties of bay grasses are found in the fresh, brackish, and salty waters of the Chesapeake Bay. Some of the most common are wild celery, sago pondweed, redhead grass, widgeon grass, and eelgrass.

The grasses grow in the sediment at the bottom of the water. Bay grasses serve many important roles. They provide food and habitat for water animals. They supply the water with oxygen. Oxygen found in water is called dissolved oxygen. Fish and other aquatic creatures use their gills to get dissolved oxygen and pass it into their bloodstream. Grasses also slow down waves to protect shorelines. They trap sediment and nutrients so that the water stays clean and clear.

CHAPTER 4

Disrupting Chesapeake Bay Grasses

In the Chesapeake Bay's natural state, bay grasses keep nutrients and sediment out of the water. This helps the rest of the hydrosphere and biosphere. But the original state of the bay's four systems was interrupted. The natural balance was upset. The grasses began to die. The health of the bay suffered.

Eelgrass, with its long, thin leaves, thrives in salty tidal water.

Algae is considered harmful if there is too much of it, or if it contains a toxin dangerous to animals and humans. Officials can close Chesapeake Bay beaches when algae comes ashore.

Polluted runoff from land has affected the water. Human activity sends foreign nutrients and sediment into the bay. This makes the water cloudy with sediment. **Algae** also benefits from the nutrients. Algae grows and clouds the water more. The water can become too cloudy. Sunlight cannot reach bay grasses. The grasses cannot live without sunlight. Since the 1950s, many grass beds have died from this problem. Eelgrass is one grass species. It once covered great areas at the bottom of the bay. Thousands of acres of the bay's eelgrass have died since the 1970s.

Bay grasses are not the only victims. Grasses create oxygen for the water, and for the fish who live there. Algae consume oxygen. Fewer grasses and too much algae cause the oxygen level to lower. There are even areas with no oxygen at all. These are called dead zoncs because plants and animals cannot live there.

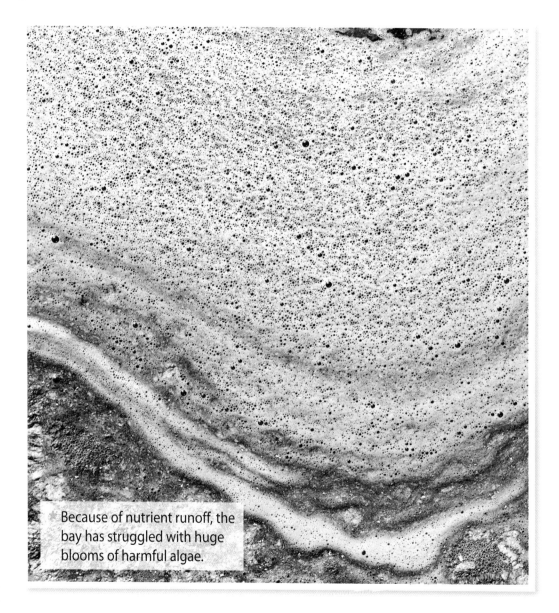

Because of nutrient runoff, the bay has struggled with huge blooms of harmful algae.

There are many **invasive species** that also threaten aquatic plants. Invasive plants such as hydrilla can spread quickly. They choke out native underwater grasses. Brazilian waterweed is native to South America. People use it in their aquariums. When they empty their aquariums, the plant ends up in the water. Brazilian waterweed grows very fast in the brackish water of the Chesapeake Bay. Thick patches of Brazilian waterweed stop the bay's water from circulating. This affects water quality, hurting native bay grasses.

* Hydrilla lives in the fresh and brackish areas of the bay. It can grow quickly and shade out other plants.

A bird called the mute swan is also a threat to native bay grasses. It can consume up to 20 pounds (9 kilograms) of the plants daily. Mute swans also chase away and even kill native birds. When bay grasses are eaten, choked out, and kept from sunlight, the health of the whole bay is at risk.

* When mute swans eat eelgrass, they tear out the entire root system, preventing it from growing more.

CHAPTER 5

Humans and the Bay

The Chesapeake Bay was named after the Algonquin word *chesepiooc*. This is said to mean "at a big river." Europeans have lived near the bay since Jamestown was settled in 1607. Humans have made many changes to the bay since then. In 1964, the Bridge-Tunnel crossed the lower bay. It is one of only 10 bridge-tunnel systems in the world and is 23 miles (37 km) long. The bay is important for shipping too. It holds two of the five biggest North Atlantic **ports** in the nation.

What Can YOU Do for the Bay?

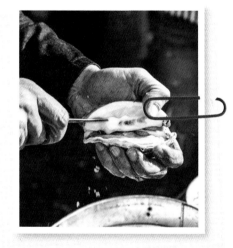

One of the biggest threats to the Chesapeake Bay is the decline of the oyster population. People who live along the bay's waters can help. Those who have piers or docks on the water can raise oyster larvae with help from local organizations. Local restaurants can recycle shucked oyster shells. These shells can be used to rebuild oyster reefs. Anyone who lives, works, or plays near the Chesapeake Bay can help oysters and other marine life by keeping trash and chemicals out of the water. Stream cleanups can prevent trash from reaching the bay. And replacing harmful chemical cleaners with natural or homemade cleaners can help keep the water safe and clean.

Farming is very important to the people of the watershed, but too much fertilizer and manure from agriculture harms the water.

Until the late 20th century, the bay was safe for marine life. It was also safe for human activities. These included commercial fishing, sailing, swimming, and sport fishing. As the population grew, humans replaced forests and wetlands with buildings and hard surfaces like pavement. Water cannot move through these hard surfaces. Runoff carries pollution from the land straight into the water. The bay's waters began to suffer.

Sewage can hurt the quality of the bay's water. Nutrients can too. Nutrients are important to the plants and animals in the bay. But too many of the wrong nutrients can change the balance of the bay's biosphere. Nutrients can come from plant fertilizers. These fertilizers are used on farms and on people's lawns. Rain washes nutrients across the hard surfaces of roads and pavement. Air pollution from cars puts the nutrients into the air, and that enters the water too.

The most harmful nutrients to the bay are nitrogen and phosphorus. Nutrient pollution is a major cause of the bay's dead zones. The Chesapeake Bay was the site of one of the earliest detected dead zones in the world, in the 1930s. The dead zone was created because of the growing human population on the shores of the bay. On the bay's west coast are cities and factories that have contributed fertilizers to runoff and nitrogen to the air. The east coast has many poultry farms that have contributed manure to the bay.

Overfishing also harms the species of the bay. Hundreds of years ago, oyster reefs were so big that it was hard for boats to steer around them. Since the late 1800s, people made millions of dollars fishing for oysters. There were once 200,000 acres (80,937 hectares) of oyster reefs. Today, there are only 36,000 acres (14,568 ha).

* The Maryland and Virginia governments set a limit on how many oysters can be harvested from Chesapeake Bay every year.

One oyster can filter more than 50 gallons (189 l) of water per day. In the late 1800s, oysters filtered the water of the entire bay every three to four days. Today, it takes the oyster population nearly a year. Fewer oysters means less clean water. This hurts all plants and animals, not just the oysters.

The bay is affected by point source pollution and nonpoint source pollution. Point source pollution is released into the air by power plants and factories. Nonpoint source pollution comes from runoff from polluted streams, or from contaminated rain or snow.

Humans rely on the Chesapeake Bay. Now the bay is relying on humans to fix its problems. The Chesapeake Bay's health has recently improved. The United States Clean Water Act of 1972 forced companies and governments to keep the water clean. The Clean Air Act of 1990 did the same for the air. These laws slowly began to help the bay. President Obama also made the government protect and restore the bay. Now the six states in the Chesapeake Bay watershed cannot pollute their water.

President Obama signed an executive order to restore the bay's health.

Global Causes, Local Effects

Local activities are not the only cause of problems in the bay. Worldwide **climate change** is also a problem. The level of the Chesapeake Bay is rising at 0.14 inches (0.36 centimeters) per year. The rising sea level affects beaches and wetlands. Water temperatures have increased almost two degrees since 1960. There is also more carbon dioxide in the atmosphere. This enters the water. Native plants and animals are hurt by these changes to the water.

Water quality has improved. Oxygen has increased. Nutrient pollution has decreased. Some of the bay's most important species are increasing. Some of these are blue crabs, striped bass, and anchovies. For the first time in many years, the nation's largest estuary has improved in every area. However, there are still many challenges ahead. Humans must not stop working to save the Chesapeake Bay.

* Blue crabs increased almost 60 percent between 2018 and 2019.

Experiment: Layers of the Bay

Introduction

Water becomes denser as it becomes saltier. This means that saltwater is heavier than freshwater.

In the estuary of the Chesapeake Bay, saltwater from the Atlantic Ocean meets freshwater from the watershed. Because they are different densities, they settle into two layers. One is a saltwater layer on the bottom. The other is a freshwater layer above.

Where the layers meet, the types mix. Mixing is also caused by wind, as well as temperature, rain, and tides. In this experiment, you will demonstrate how saltwater and freshwater layer and mix in the Chesapeake Bay, and how wind can affect this.

Materials:

* Measuring cup
* Tap water
* 3 teaspoons (14.3 grams) of salt
* Spoon
* Straw
* Red and blue food coloring
* Two clear cups

Instructions:

1. In your measuring cup, mix the salt into 1/2 cup (118 milliliters) of water. Use your spoon to stir and dissolve the salt into the water. When it is dissolved, you will not see grains of salt in the water.

2. Add 3 drops of blue food coloring to the measuring cup. Pour the blue, salty water into one of your clear cups. Rinse the measuring cup.

3. Fill your rinsed measuring cup with 1/2 cup (118 ml) of freshwater. Add 3 drops of red food coloring.

4. Very slowly pour the red freshwater down the side of the cup into the blue saltwater. What happened? Why do you think this happened?

5. Now put your straw at an angle near the surface of the water. Blow very lightly with your straw. Try blowing harder, or at a different angle. What happened to the water? Why do you think this happened?

6. Now reverse the experiment. Pour the freshwater into the clear cup first. Then very slowly pour the saltwater down the side. What happened? Why do you think this happened?

Explanation:

In the first experiment, you should have seen two obvious layers of water form. The red freshwater should have floated on top of the blue saltwater because it is less dense (lighter).

When you blew on the surface, you should have seen some mixing occur. This represents how wind can affect the mixing of the bay's layers.

In the reversed experiment, you should have observed swirls of saltwater sinking to the bottom of the cup. This is similar to the estuary's current.

Remember that cold water is denser and heavier than warm water. So cold water tends to sink. What do you think might happen in this experiment if the freshwater were colder than the saltwater?

Glossary

airshed *(AIR-shed)* region of air above the bay

algae *(AL-jee)* plant-like organism that has no roots, stems, or leaves

anadromous *(uh-NAD-ruh-mihs)* fish that live in the ocean but swim into rivers or streams to lay eggs

atmosphere *(AT-muhs-feer)* part of the planet made of air

biosphere *(BYE-oh-sfeer)* part of the planet made of living things

brackish *(BRAK-ish)* water made up of saltwater and river water

climate change *(KLYE-mit CHAYNJ)* long-term change in the Earth's weather patterns

denser *(DEN-sur)* more compacted

estuary *(EHS-choo-air-ee)* area where a river or tributary meets the ocean

geosphere *(JEE-oh-sfeer)* part of the planet made of solid ground

glaciers *(GLAY-shurz)* huge areas of very thick ice that flow slowly over land

habitats *(HAB-ih-tats)* natural environments where a plant or animal lives

hydrosphere *(HYE-droh-sfeer)* part of the planet made of water

invasive species *(in-VAY-siv SPEE-sheez)* plants or animals that are not native to an area and cause harm to other species in that area

migrating *(MYE-gray-ting)* moving from one habitat or region to another according to the season

nutrients *(NOO-tree-ints)* important chemicals that are necessary for all living things

pollution *(puh-LOO-shin)* when the air, land, or water is dirtied by chemicals, waste, or other harmful things

ports *(POHRTS)* where ships dock to load and unload

predatory *(PREH-duh-toh-ree)* relating to animals who naturally hunt and eat other animals

runoff *(RUN-ahf)* the draining of water off land and into a body of water

sediment *(SED-ih-ment)* stones or sand carried in water

sewage *(soo-ihj)* human waste and wastewater, carried in underground pipes

shellfish *(SHEL-fish)* sea creatures with hard shells

wetlands *(WET-lands)* land that is saturated with water, such as marshes and swamps

For More Information

Books

Heitkamp, Kristina Lyn. *The Water Cycle.* New York, NY: Britannica Educational Publishing, 2018.

Herman, Gail. *What Is Climate Change?* New York, NY: Penguin, 2018.

Simmer, Yuval and Barbara Taylor. *The Big Book of the Blue.* New York, NY: Thames & Hudson, 2018.

Websites

Ducksters Education Site
https://www.ducksters.com/science/earth_science
Find kid-friendly information about earth science and related subjects.

eSchool Today
http://eschooltoday.com/pollution/water-pollution/what-is-water-pollution.html
Learn basic facts about water pollution.

Chesapeake Bay Program
https://www.chesapeakebay.net/discover/bay-101
Discover details about the Chesapeake Bay, problems facing it, and what people are doing to help.

Index

About the Author

Leah Kaminski lives in Chicago with her husband and son. She has written other books for children, about science, geography, and culture. Leah also writes poetry, often about the natural environment—so she loves learning more about everything related to science and ecology.